COOL
Animal
Names

COOL Animal Names

Porcupinefish, Zebra Eels,
Leopard Geckos, Owl Monkeys,
Giraffe Beetles, & 251 other
BIZARRE Creatures

DAWN CUSICK

imagine!
Publishing

An Imagine Book
Published by Charlesbridge
85 Main Street
Watertown, MA 02472
(617) 926-0329
www.charlesbridge.com

Library of Congress Cataloging-in-Publication Data
Cusick, Dawn.
Cool animal names : porcupine fish, zebra eels, leopard geckos, owl monkeys, giraffe beetles, & 251 other bizarre creatures / Dawn Cusick.
   p. cm.
Includes index.
ISBN 978-1-936140-39-8
1. Animals—Nomenclature (Popular)—Juvenile literature. I. Title.
QL355.C87 2011
591—dc22

                                             2011009637

Printed in China. Manufactured in April, 2011.

(hc) 10 9 8 7 6 5 4 3 2 1

Display type and text type set in Gotham Book and AdLib.

Designed by Susan McBride
Jacket Design by Celia Naranjo
Copy Editing by Catherine Ham
Produced by EarlyLight Books

For information about custom editions, special sales, premium and corporate purchases, please contact Charlesbridge Publishing at specialsales@charlesbridge.com

• •

To my parents, Joyce & Gene Cusick

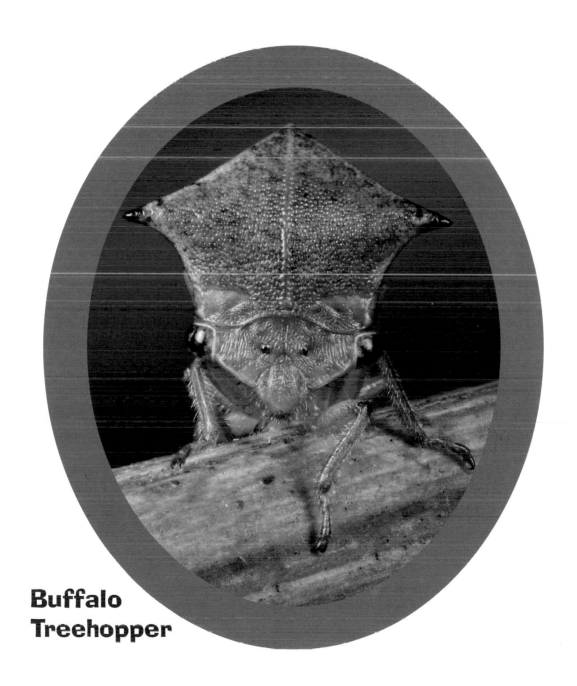

Buffalo Treehopper

CONTENTS

Ruby Tiger Moth

Alligator Snapping Turtle

Pigfish

Zebra Eel

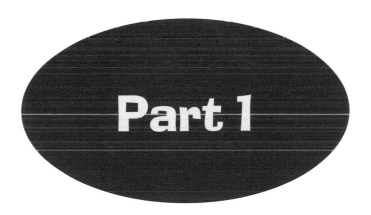

Part 1

Welcome to the wild and wacky world of Cool Animal Names!

Before you turn the page, get your brain ready to play. Check out the animal pictures on the left page, then close your eyes and imagine an alligator turtle, a squirrel monkey, a parrot snake, a skunk beetle, a tiger salamander, a fox shark, and a scorpion fly. Pretty bizarre pictures, aren't they?

When you're ready for more, you will meet tiger snails, zebra fish, and many other cool animals!

Tigers

are the largest cats in the world. They live in China, Russia, and some other parts of Asia. Three types of tigers have gone extinct, and the remaining six types are endangered.

Tiger stripes can be grey, brown, or black. These stripes help tigers blend in with their environment. Hiding is important for tigers because they are ambush predators and catch prey by sneaking up on them. All tigers have stripes, but the stripe pattern on every tiger is different.

`TIGER`
`STRIPES`

`TIGER`

Tiger Snakes

(right) are a type of cobra with circular bands of black and yellow stripes that look like tiger stripes. They eat small birds, small mammals, and frogs.

Tiger- Legged Monkey Tree Frogs

(above) live near small ponds in India and Pakistan. Adult tiger-legged monkey tree frogs do not look like tigers, but their tadpoles behave like them! The tadpoles have two rows of teeth with strong jaws, and are good hunters.

Ruby Tiger Moths

(right) are a reddish-brown tiger moth with brushy tufts around their heads. There are more than 10,000 species (types) of tiger moths! See more tiger moths on page 17.

Tiger Salamanders

(left) spend their days in burrows in the ground to keep their skin moist. At night, they come out of their burrows to hunt bugs, worms, and small frogs. Tiger salamanders were named for their yellow spots and stripes. There are several types of tiger salamander. The salamander on the left is an Eastern tiger salamander; the one on the far left is a mottled tiger salamander.

Tiger Pythons

(right) are a type of python with tiger-like patterns on their scales. The snake shown here is a purple tiger albino.

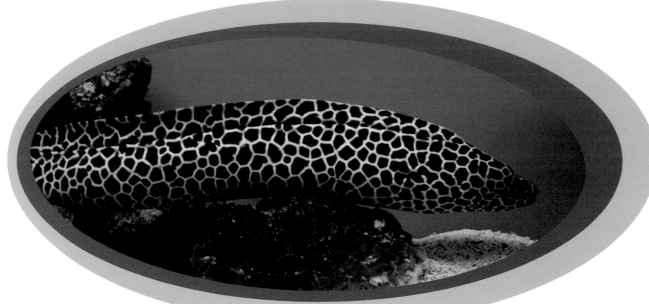

Tiger Eels

(above) live in the oceans near Australia and Africa. Their bodies are covered with black spots. They spend most of their time hiding, covered in sand, but come out to hunt small fish.

Tiger Shrimp

(above) were named for their large size and their black stripes. They are found off the coasts of China, Japan, India, Thailand, Korea, and East Africa. Tiger Shrimp are a popular menu item in many restaurants.

Tiger Sharks

(left) have both spots and stripes. They also have big eyes and big mouths. They are one of the few types of sharks known to attack people, but this may be because they hunt for fish in shallow waters where people swim and snorkel.

Tiger Oscar Fish

(right) hunt for small fish, worms, insect larvae, and crayfish on the muddy bottoms of South American rivers. They are popular with people who keep fish as pets because they come to the edge of their tanks when people are near. Tiger Oscar fish are now found in some areas of Australia and North America, probably because pet owners have released them into the wild.

Tiger Cardinalfish

(left) were named after both tigers and birds! The tiger part of their name comes from their stripes, while the bird part of their name comes from their red coloring, which is similar to that of male cardinal birds.

Tiger Groupers

(right) are ambush predators that hide in rocky areas in coral reefs, waiting for small fish to swim by. Their tiger-like stripes help conceal them, making it easier to surprise an unsuspecting fish. Tiger groupers are found in the warm waters off the coast of Florida in North America and in parts of South America.

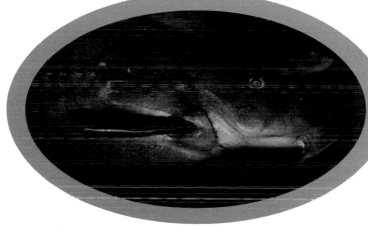

Tiger Shovelnose Catfish

(left) live in South American lakes and rivers. They hunt at night for small fish, crabs, and shrimp. They have very large barbels, which they use to help find food in the dark.

Tiger Herons

(left) live near rivers and lakes in Mexico and Central America, where they hunt for fish, crabs, and frogs. Tiger herons were named for the tiger-like sound of their calls.

Tiger Snails

(below) live in swamps along the coast of East Africa. Their orange and black stripes probably inspired their name. One type of tiger snail, the giant Ghana tiger, is the largest land snail on earth.

Tiger Bengal Cats

are a type of domesticated cat that has been bred with an Asian leopard cat. They have tiger-like stripes and leopard-like spots.

Tiger Flatworms

(right) live in warm Tropical oceans. They were named for their tiger-like stripes and coloring. Their bodies are very thin, and they get oxygen through their skin instead of with gills or lungs.

Tiger Tarantulas

(left) live in South America. They have orange stripes on their legs and their abdomens. They are good climbers and fast runners.

Tiger Leeches

(above) live in Malaysia. They were named for their bright red-orange coloring and stripes, which may help them blend in with the fur of the animals they feed on. Camouflage is important for tiger leeches because some birds spend a lot of time searching for them.

TIGER CUB

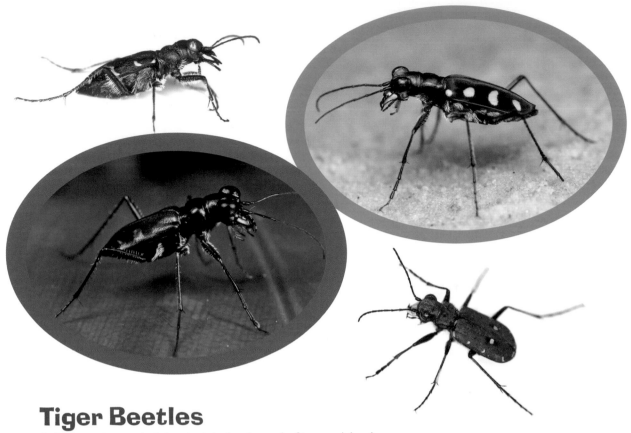

Tiger Beetles

(above, top right, right, below left, and below right) were named after tigers because they are fast, fierce predators. They eat small insects and spiders, and can be found in most areas of the world. There are more than 2,300 species (types) of tiger beetles, and many of them have shiny, brightly colored bodies.

Water Tigers

(left) are a type of beetle named because they are predators in streams, lakes, ponds, and rivers. Because they can hunt under water, they are also called diving beetles.

Tiger Swallowtails

(left) are a type of butterfly known for their tiger-like colors and stripes. When they are caterpillars (right) the head area of their bodies develops fake eyes that frighten predators.

Tiger Moths

(below, and below right) have stripe patterns on their wings, and orange and black coloring that reminds people of tigers. When they are caterpillars, tiger moths are covered with hair, do not have stripes, and are called wooly bears.

Scarlet Tigers

(above) are a type of tiger moth found in parts of Asia and Europe. Their underwings are a bright scarlet color.

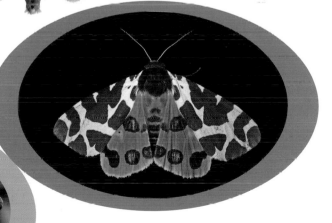

Tiger Butterflies

(left) were named for their orange color and their black stripes.

Leopards

are large, wild cats that live in Africa, India, and Asia. They are ambush predators and their spotted coats help them blend in with trees and tall grasses, making it easier to sneak up on prey.

A leopard's spots are solid black on their head, neck, chest, and legs. In other places, the spots are arranged in flower-like clusters called rosettes. In many parts of the world, leopards are hunted and killed for their coats.

LEOPARD

Leopard Frogs

(above) live in shallow streams and ponds. Their spots help them blend in with plants.

Leopard Seals

live and hunt in the icy waters of the Antarctic. Their fur has a spotted pattern, and they have very sharp teeth for catching prey.

Leopard Geckos

(left) live in rocky desert areas. When they are young, they have stripes around their bodies. As they grow larger, the stripes break into spots.

Leopard Sharks

hunt for prey on shallow ocean floors when they are young. The spots help them hide against the sandy bottom as they search for mollusks, worms, small fish, and other small sea animals. As they get older, leopard sharks move to deeper water and lose their distinctive spots.

Leopard Moths

(below) are black and fuzzy when they are caterpillars. When they are adults, they have white wings with black spots.

Leopard Tortoises

live in the woodlands and savannas of Africa. They are named for the spots on their shells. When some leopard tortoises hibernate, they bury all of their bodies except for the top of their shell underground, and their spots help them blend in with grass.

Zebras

are close relatives of horses, and are found in Africa. Biologists believe their camouflaging stripes protect zebras in several ways. The stripes help them blend into the tall grasses or into other members of a herd so large predators such as lions have trouble seeing them. A zebra's stripes may also confuse blood-sucking parasites.

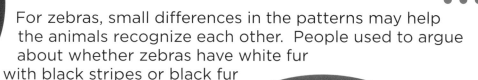

For zebras, small differences in the patterns may help the animals recognize each other. People used to argue about whether zebras have white fur with black stripes or black fur with white stripes. The debate ended when biologists discovered zebras have dark fur.

Zebra Butterflies

have black stripes on a pale yellow background. They often fly in groups, and the moving stripes make it hard for predators to know exactly where they are.

Zebra Sharks

Is it a shark? Is it a zebra? It's a shark that looks like a zebra! Zebra sharks only have stripes when they're young. Once they become adults, their stripes turn to spots, and they're often mistakenly called leopard sharks.

Zebra Finches

originally came from Australia and parts of Indonesia. Males have black and white stripes around their faces, on their chests, and on their tail feathers. Females are much less colorful, and don't have chest stripes.

Zebrafish

sport zebra-like stripes on their scales. They live in southern Asia, but are kept as pets in aquariums around the world. Check out pages 67 & 76 to discover more fish named after zebras.

Zebra Spiders

(below) are a type of jumping spider named for their stripes. Zebra spiders do not build webs, They have two large eyes and six smaller eyes to help them find prey. The zebra tarantula (right) is hairy and scary, but you won't see one unless you go to Costa Rica or a zoo.

Zebra Mice

come from Africa, where their stripes help them blend in with plants while they search for fruits and seeds.

Zebra Moray Eels

(above right) are dark brown with thin white stripes that encircle their bodies. During the day, zebra moray eels hide under rocks and in crevices of coral reefs. At night, they hunt for clams, crabs, and sea urchins.

Elephants

are the largest mammals found on land. They live in Africa and Asia, and are on the Endangered Species' List. Elephants are well known for their distinctive trunks, which can grow more than 7 feet long!

Elephants use their trunks in many ways. To get food, they wrap their trunks around branches, pulling the leaves down to their mouths. To make sounds, they force air through their long trunks.

ELEPHANT

Elephant Seals

are the largest seals in the world. They were named after elephants because the males have a large nose that looks like an elephant's trunk. Males make loud, drum-like sounds from their noses by blowing air into them, and use the noise to threaten other males.

Elephant Beetles

Above: See page 50 to learn about elephant beetles.

Elephant Sharks

Right: See page 63 to learn about elephant sharks.

Elephant Shrews

(below) were named for their long, trunk-like noses, which they use to search for insects to eat.

Elephant Ear Coral

(above) might look like mushrooms, but they're really many small animals living together. They are close relatives of jellyfish.

Elephant Hawk Moths

(left) were so named because their larval forms, caterpillars, look like an elephant's trunk. They live in many parts of Europe. Adult moths are bright pink and green.

Peacocks

are tall pheasant birds. Males have large, colorful tails with bright eyespots on them. Eyespots are areas that look like eyes and may be used to scare away predators. Females have much smaller tails and do not have eyespots.

PEACOCK

EYESPOTS

Peacock Hinds

live in the Red Sea near coral reefs, where their spots may help them blend in. They are also called blue-spotted grouper and peacock rockcod. They eat small fish.

Peacock Flounders

are named after peacocks because they are covered in spots. Some people think the spots look like flowers and call them flower flounders.

Peacock flounders spend their days hiding on sandy ocean bottoms so they can catch small shrimp, fish, and crabs for dinner.

Peacock Frogs

are also called peacock tree frogs and big-eyed tree frogs. They live in trees in Tanzania. Young frogs are bright green, while adults develop some brown spots.

Peacock Mantis Shrimp

(right and below) have bright colors and a large, bright tail, as peacocks do. They were also named after the praying mantis because of the way they stalk their prey.

Peacock Mantids

(left) do not look anything like peacocks when they are resting or hunting. When they feel threatened, though, they open up their wings to reveal big eyespots that scare away predators!

Peacock Moths

(above and below) live in Asia and Europe. They are named for the large eyespot found in the middle of each wing. Peacock moth caterpillars also have spots, but look very different as adults.

Rhinos

are related to horses and zebras. There are five different species (types) of rhinoceros (called rhinos for short) living in Asia, India, and Africa. Male rhinos use their horns to fight other males, to fight off predators, and like a shovel to dig in the ground. All rhinos are endangered.

The word rhino means "horn-nosed," and animals named after rhinos have horns of some kind.

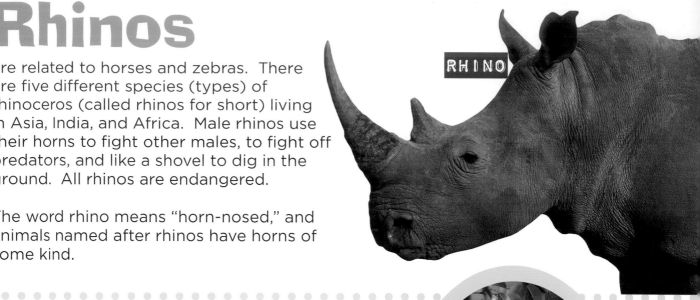

Rhinoceros Iguanas

(below) live on Caribbean islands. Males have three large horns on their heads and spines running down their backs. The horns and spines may help them attract females.

Rhinoceros Hornbills

(above right) live in Asia. They were named for the large, rhino-like horn on the top of their beaks, which is called a casque, and biologists are not sure whether it's used to make their calls louder or as a weapon in fights.

Rhinoceros Vipers

(left) have large, horn-like scales on the end of their snouts that look like rhino horns. They live near rivers in African rain forests and are also called River Jacks.

Camels

are large mammals that live in deserts. Camels from Asia have one hump, while camels from Africa and the Middle East have two. Many people believe that camels store water in their humps, but the humps actually store fat.

Camels have long eyelashes and bushy eyebrows to help keep sand out of their eyes. They can also close their nostrils, which keeps sand out of their noses during sandstorms. If you concentrate really hard, can you do that?

CAMEL

Camel Crickets

(above) were named for the hump-like curve to the upper part of their bodies. Camel crickets are also called cave crickets.

Camel Spiders

Below: See page 44 to learn about camel spiders.

Camel Cowfish

(above) were named after both camels and cows. The camel part of their name comes from the hump-like bulge on their backs, while the cow part of their name comes from the horn-like protrusions on the front of their heads. They are also called thornback boxfish. To learn more about cowfish, see page 66.

Squirrels

are small mammals with big, bushy tails and large eyes. Although they are well known for their ability to leap from branch to branch in tall trees, not all squirrels live in trees. Some squirrels live on the ground, while others live underground in burrows.

There are more than 200 species (types) of squirrels, and their strong teeth help them eat nuts, tree bark, and roots.

SQUIRREL

Squirrel Monkeys

live in South and Central American rainforests. They spend their days leaping from tree to tree, the way squirrels do. They talk to each other with noises that sound like whistles and squeaks.

Squirrelfish

have large eyes, just like squirrels, and use them at night to hunt for small fish and crabs. During the day, squirrelfish hide in caves or under reef rocks.

Skunks

are medium-sized mammals known for the bad-smelling liquid they spray on animals as a defense. The spray comes from under their tails, and can travel as far as 10 feet! Often skunks do not have to spray a predator — they only have to raise their tails as a warning.

Animals named after skunks may use foul smells to defend themselves or have skunk-like stripes.

SKUNK

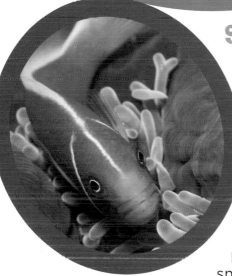

Skunk Bears

(left) look like small bears but are actually a type of weasel. They were named after skunks because of the skunk-like odors they use to mark their territories. They are also called wolverines.

Skunk Clownfish

Left: See page 77 to learn about skunk clownfish.

Skunk Beetles

(right) defend themselves by standing on their heads and spraying predators with a bad-smelling liquid from their hind ends.

Bats

are the only mammals capable of true flight. A membrane stretched between their long finger bones works like bird wings. Although bats are often portrayed as blood-suckers in scary movies, only a few bat species feed on blood — instead, most bats eat insects, fruit, and flower nectar.

BAT

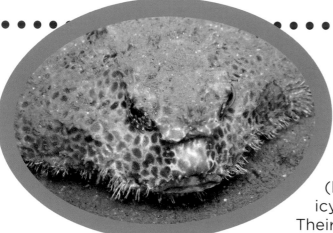

Batfish

(left) live and hunt in the icy waters of the Antarctic. Their scales have a spotted pattern that helps them hide, and they have very sharp teeth for catching prey.

Bat Rays

(below) are a type of stingray with wide pectoral fins that look like a flying bat when they swim. Bat rays use their fins to move sand on the ocean floor while searching for dinner clams.

Bat Sea Stars

(right) were named after bats because the webbing between their arms looks like the webbing between bat fingers.

Rats

Many people do not like these close relatives of hamsters and mice. Their large teeth, long whiskers, and skinny tails are often featured in cartoons and scary movies. A rat's tail is pretty amazing. It does not have hair on it, and rats are able to enlarge or shrink the blood vessels in their long tails to add or take away heat from their bodies!

RAT

Rat Snakes

are not poisonous, and are common in the southern United States. Adult snakes eat rats, mice, birds, and bird eggs, and are different colors, depending on where they live. live. All young snakes (juveniles) have rat-like coloring.

Rat Kangaroos

(below) live in Australia and Tasmania, and are often described as looking just like a really big rat! They have long legs, long ears, and a long, rat-like tail.

Ratfish

spend most of their time on the sandy bottom of ocean floors, and are relatives of stingrays and skates. They were named after rats because of their long, rat-like tails and their large, protruding front teeth that are used for crushing crabs and clamshells.

Cats & Dogs

come in all shapes and sizes, with lots of variation in their personalities. Many large wild cats, such as lions and tigers, are endangered species. Other cats, such as the domesticated house cat, have made wonderful pets for almost 10,000 years. Some people estimate there are more than 400 million dogs in the world — that's a lot of dogs!

CAT

DOG

Catfish

Below: See page 73 to learn about catfish.

Cat-Bears

(below) are also called red pandas and bear cats. They are relatives of panda bears, and were named after cats for their pupil shapes, which are vertical, like cat pupils.

Catbirds

(left) were named after cats because parts of their song sound like a cat's meow. Catbirds spend much of their time searching for insects and fruit on the ground.

Dog Ticks

(below) a species (type) of tick that is often found on dogs. If you take a quick look at a dog tick, you might think it's a bug, but ticks are actually closely related to spiders. They have eight legs, not six, and two body segments.

Dogfish Sharks

are named after dogs because they often hunt in packs, eating every fish they can find.

Dog-Faced Pufferfish

(right) live in the Indian and Pacific oceans, often near coral reefs. They were named for their dog-like look. People who keep fish as pets often like to have them in their home aquariums.

Cat Sharks

(left) make up a group of more than 110 sharks called the cat shark family. Cat sharks were named after cats because their eyes have a vertical shape, like a cat's pupils. Surprisingly, some species in the group are called dogfish! Cat sharks also have whisker-like barbels, like catfish do.

Alligators

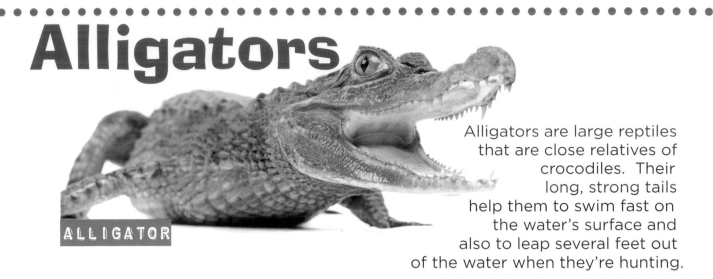

ALLIGATOR

Alligators are large reptiles that are close relatives of crocodiles. Their long, strong tails help them to swim fast on the water's surface and also to leap several feet out of the water when they're hunting.

Alligator Lizards

(below left) look like small alligators. They are good swimmers and good hunters, often eating other lizards, spiders, and insects. When they feel threatened by a predator, they open their mouths wide and show their teeth.

Alligator Bugs

(right and far right) were named for the long, snout-like shapes of their heads. They live in Belize, and are also called peanutbugs and lantern bugs.

Alligator Snapping Turtles

are one of the largest freshwater turtles in the world. They are well known for the worm-like growth they have on the tip of their tongue. To catch fish, they lie very still with their mouths open. When a fish comes over to eat the tasty worm, they become dinner for the alligator turtle!

Snakes

are long, slender reptiles without external arms or legs whose bodies are covered in scales. They are found almost everywhere in the world. Some species inject poison when they bite, but most do not. Although many people are afraid of snakes and think they are slimy, their skin is actually very smooth.

SNAKE

Snakeflies

(above) were named for their long, thin necks that look like snakes. (Technically, insects do not have necks, but the snakefly's elongated head segment looks like a neck.) Adult snakeflies have wings but do not fly well.

Snakeheads

(below) were named for their snake-like heads. They live in Asia, but are considered invasive species in North American waters.

Snakeheads can take gulps of air on the water's surface, and can live out of water for several days if their scales are kept moist.

Snake Eels

(below) live in oceans around the world and were named for the snake-like shape of their bodies.

Snake-Birds

(right) earned their name because their long, curved necks and pointed beaks look like a snake when they're hunting for fish. Their beaks have a sharp edge that is serrated like a steak knife, which helps them spear fish.

Wolves

are large members of the canine family and are close relatives of our wonderful family pets, dogs.

Long ago, wolves lived in many parts of the world, but in some places they were hunted by humans.

Wolves live and hunt in groups called packs. Their pups are born in dens and are cared for by many members of the pack.

WOLF

Wolf Eels

(right) are a type of fish named for their eel-like body shapes. They spend their days hiding in caves from predators and their nights hunting for food.

Wolf Guenon Monkeys

(above) do not look or hunt like wolves. In fact, these African monkeys eat fruits, nuts, leaves, and insects. So why is the word wolf in their name? They were named after the person who discovered them, whose last name was Wolf.

Wolf Spiders

(left and right) were named for the the wolf-like way they stalk their prey. Instead of spinning webs, wolf spiders ambush their prey. Female wolf spiders are known for being good moms. After their eggs hatch, they carry their tiny spiderlings around on their abdomens until they are big enough to care for themselves.

Scorpions

are close relatives of spiders and ticks. The tips of their tails have stingers on them that inject a painful venom that can sometimes cause death. There are more than 1400 species (types) of scorpions living in deserts and forests on every continent except Antarctica.

Scorpionflies

are large, predatory insects with two pairs of wings. (True flies, the Diptera, only have one pair of wings.) When the males curve their abdomens upward, it looks like they have a scorpion's tail!

Scorpionfish

live in warm-water oceans near the United States. They use the tips of their poisonous fins to defend themselves against larger predators. Look for more scorpionfish on page 69.

Spiders

are arthropods that are related to insects and crabs. Many people are afraid of spiders and associate them with Halloween and scary movies. When people think of spiders, they often think about species that live in webs, inject venom when they bite, or are covered in brown or black hair.

Actually, not all spiders bite, and many spiders don't spin webs. Not all spiders have hair, and some are brightly colored with amazing patterns.

SPIDER

Spider Conchs

are a type of snail that lives under water. A large, muscular foot helps them find food and move from place to place. Spider conchs were named after spiders because of the spider-like legs of their shells.

Spider Crabs

(above and right) come in all sizes, from smaller than your pinkie fingernail to a type in Japan that is larger than a car! Spider crabs were named after spiders because of their long, thin, legs.

Spider Tortoises

(below) are small turtles named for the yellow pattern on their shells that look like spider webs. They live in Madagascar, a large island off the coast of Africa.

Spider Monkey

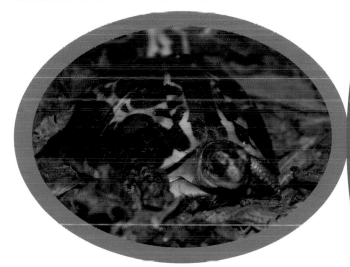

Spider Wasps

(below) do not look like spiders at all. So why were they named after them? When a female spider wasp is ready to lay an egg, she stings a spider, carries it back to her nest, and lays an egg on the spider's body. When the young wasp comes out of its egg, dinner is waiting!

Spider Monkeys

(right and above right) were named after spiders because they look like spiders when they swing from tree to tree by their tails in forests. Their tails are so strong that they can use their hands to get food while hanging upside down!

Giraffe

Giraffe Beetle

Part 2

Here we go again! Believe it or not, there are all kinds of animals with Cool Animal Names!

Some types of animals have an amazing number of species named after other animals. When you get to the beetle pages, for instance, you will find tortoise beetles, elephant beetles, tiger beetles, zebra beetles, and rhino beetles, not to mention the great giraffe beetle shown here. Any guesses how the giraffe beetle got its name?

Once you have looked through dozens of fish named after animals (pigfish, cowfish, crocodilefish, porcupinefish, and so many more), be sure to play the Name Games on page 78.

Spiders

There are more than 50,000 species (types) of spiders in the world, and only a few have bites that can hurt humans.

Spiders spin silk from a special place in the back of their bodies called a spinneret. Females wrap this silk around their eggs to help protect them, and newly hatched spiders use their silk like a parachute to move to safe places. Not all spiders catch their prey in webs; some are ambush predators, instead!

SPIDER

Mouse Spiders

(below) live in Australia and were named after mice because they dig mouse-like burrows. They cover the burrow's opening with a silk web, then eat the insects that fall in. They have large fangs and toxic venom.

Wolf Spiders

(above) do not spin webs. Instead, they go hunting at night and stalk their prey, the way wolves do. You may see wolf spiders in your house when they go looking for warm places during the winter. They are not venomous.

Baboon Spiders

are also called baboon tarantulas, and are the spiders seen in lots of scary movies. They were named after baboons because some people think the ends of their legs look like baboon fingers. They use their legs and fangs to dig in the ground, and they like to eat crickets and roaches.

Crab   Spiders

(below) were named because they move sideways and backward like crabs do. Instead of spinning webs, they hide on flowers and surprise their prey. How long do you think you could sit still to catch your dinner? For hours, the way a crab spider can?

Ant Crab Spiders

(above) are a type of crab spider that mimics (looks like) an ant. You can tell whether you are looking at a crab spider or an ant by watching them move and counting their legs. An ant crab spider moves sideways, like a crab, not forward, like an ant. It also has four pairs of legs like all other spiders, not three pairs, like insects.

Zebra Tarantulas

(above) have zebra-like stripes. Their favorite foods are cockroaches, but they will also eat other small insects such as crickets and grasshoppers.

Wasp Spiders

(above) were named for the yellow and black, wasp-like stripes found on the females. The males do not look like wasps at all — they are light brown!

Zebra Spiders

(above) are a type of jumping spider named for their zebra-like stripes formed with black and white hairs.

Camel Spiders

(above) live in deserts in the Far East and eat small lizards, scorpions, and bugs. They are also called sun spiders and sand spiders.

Moths

MOTH

are close relatives of butterflies. Like butterflies, they begin their lives as eggs, then hatch into larvae (usually called caterpillars). The caterpillars spend most of their time eating. Before changing into an adult moth, they spin a cocoon or form a chrysalis, and go into their pupal stage where they finish developing.

Moths usually fly at night, while butterflies fly during the day. They tend to have plump and hairy bodies, while butterflies are more slender and tend to be hairless.

Fox Moths

(right) were named after foxes because the males are a reddish-brown color, similar to the color of fox fur. They live near oceans and bogs, and are very fast fliers.

Tiger Moths

(below) have stripes on their abdomens that look like tiger stripes. See page 17 to discover more about tiger moths.

Elephant Hawk Moths

(above) were named because the caterpillars look like an elephant's trunk. See page 23 to find more about elephant hawk moths.

Cobra Moths

(below) are named after cobras because some people think the tips of their wings look like snake heads. Can you see snake heads on the wings? Female cobra moths lay their eggs on the underside of leaves.

Leopard Moths

(below) are a type of tiger moth that have open black spots on their white wings, similar to leopard spots. Farmers dislike leopard moths because the caterpillars eat through the stems of their fruit trees, causing lots of damage.

Lobster Moths

(above) look nothing like lobsters when they are adults, but the caterpillars have curled-back tails that remind some people of lobster tails.

Peacock Moths

were named for the large eyespot found in the middle of each wing. See page 25 to learn more about peacock moths.

Other Moths Named after Animals:

Sheep Moths, Kitten Moths, Goat Moths, Grasshopper Moths, & Robin Moths

Bee
Hawk Moths

(right) moths were named for their short, bee-like body and the humming sound their wings make.

Hummingbird Moths

(below) were named after hummingbirds because their wings make a humming sound when they hover near flowers. Hummingbird moths also have long tongues, just like hummingbirds, which they use to suck nectar from flowers.

Hawk Moths

(above) are a group of moths that are strong flyers, like hawk birds. They use their powerful wings to help them hover while sucking nectar from flower blooms.

Flies

True flies are in the order Diptera and have two long wings adapted for flight. House flies are true flies, and so are crane flies and mosquitoes. Many other insects have the word "fly" in their name, probably because they move from one place to another by flying.

FLY

Horse Flies

(left) are true flies known for biting both horses and humans. They often have very colorful eyes.

Snakeflies

(below right) were named for their long, thin necks that look like snakes. (Technically, insects do not have necks, but the snakefly's extra-long head segment looks like a neck.) Adult snake flies have wings but do not fly well.

Snipe Flies

(above) are closely related to horse and deer flies. They are known for their interesting habit of facing downward on trees, and have been called "down-looking" flies. Both snipe flies and snipe birds are often found in wetland areas, which may be how the fly got its name.

Scorpionflies

(right) are large, predatory insects. They have two pairs of wings, not one, so they are not true flies. They are named after scorpions because when the males curve their abdomens upward, it looks like a scorpion's tail! Check out another scorpionfly picture on page 37.

Owlflies

(above) may have been named after owls because of their large eyes. They are true flies, but are related to dragonflies and ant lions. Owlflies are fierce predators, feasting on other insects every chance they get!

Deer Flies

(left) are large brown flies that live near deer and other large mammals. Only the females bite, and their bites cause swelling, infection, and sometimes disease.

Beetle Flies

(right) look like beetles because of the shiny, beetle-like covering on their backs. There are about 90 species (types) of beetle flies, and they are found in Asia and Africa.

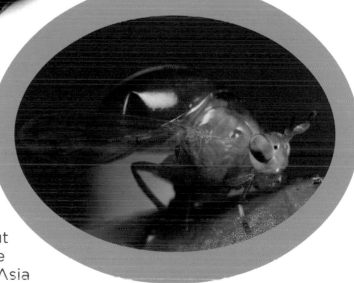

Beetles

are amazing insects. Their front wings harden into a protective covering that works like armor. Beetles are found almost everywhere on earth, and there are more than 340,000 known species (types).

BEETLE

Beetles are important members of ecosystems because they break down dead plants and animals, which helps to make healthy soil. Many species of beetles are disliked by farmers because they eat their crops.

Flea Beetles

(right) are small beetles that live on fruits and vegetables. They have long back legs that help them jump — just like fleas — when they want to move or when a predator disturbs them.

Elephant Beetles

(right) are also called ox beetles, and were named after elephants because males have three horns on their heads, two that are short and one that is very long, like a trunk. Males use these horns for fighting. Females have small bumps on their heads instead of horns.

Giraffe Beetles

(above right) live in Madagascar. The males have long necks, similar to giraffes. They use their long necks to help them build nests.

Tiger Beetles

(right) were named after tigers because they are fast, fierce predators, just like tigers. Even tiger beetles in the larval stage are strong hunters! There are more than 2,000 species of tiger beetles.

Rhinoceros Beetles

(above) use their large horns to search through leaves, dig holes, and fight other rhinoceros beetles and predators. Rhinoceros beetles are close relatives of elephant beetles.

Skunk Beetles

(left) defend themselves by standing on their heads and spraying predators with a bad-smelling liquid from their hind ends. Grasshoppers, skunks, and mice are big predators of skunk beetles.

Tortoise Beetles

(above right) were named after tortoises because their bodies are shaped like a tortoise shell. They stay warm under leaves in the winter; in the summer, sweet potatoes are their favorite food.

Frogs

are cold-blooded amphibians that usually lay their eggs near ponds or lakes. Amphibians are related to reptiles but they do not have scales. Frog eggs hatch into tadpoles, which live in water for several months while they develop into frogs. The World Conservation Union says that at least one-third of all amphibians are endangered.

Pig Frogs

make loud, grunting noises similar to—can you guess? PIGS! Pig frogs have narrow, pointed heads, and spend much of their time around lakes and ponds.

Tiger-Legged Monkey Frogs

Right: Learn about this animal on page 10.

Cricket Frogs

(above) were named after crickets because male cricket frogs sound like singing crickets when they call to attract females. Cricket frogs are good jumpers, which is a good thing because birds, snakes, and fish like to eat them!

Monkey Frogs

(right) are a type of tree frog with long fingers and toes, which they use to wrap around tree limbs to help them hold on, the way monkeys do.

Squirrel Tree Frogs

(left) were named after squirrels because the males' calls sound like squirrels. They spend their days resting in the shade, and hunt for bugs and mates at night.

Leopard Frogs

(below) live in shallow streams and ponds. Their spots usually have light-colored circles around them, and help the frogs blend in with plants.

Peacock Frogs

(left) are also called peacock tree frogs and big-eyed tree frogs. They live in trees in Tanzania. Young frogs are bright green, while adults have brown spots.

Owls

cannot see very well close up, but can see their prey very well in the distance, even in darkness. Some species (types) of owls are smaller than your hand, while others are as big as an eagle.

Owls that hunt at night and sleep during the day often have feather colors that help them blend in with the colors of the   trees they sleep in.

OWL

Rat Owls

(right) are also known as barn owls, ghost owls, and monkey-faced owls. They like to eat rats!

Goat Owls

(below) were named after goats because people used to think they drank goat milk! Goat owls are not technically owls, but may have been named after owls because they are active at night. They are also called nightjars.

Hawk Owls

(left) were named after hawks because they look and act like hawks. They hunt the same way hawks do, swooping down from high perches to catch prey. Hawk owls eat small mammals, fish, birds, and frogs.

Eagle Owls

(above and left) are the largest of all the owls. They were named after eagles because they live in the same places eagles live. If you see an eagle owl flying in the sky above you, their large wingspan makes them look a flying eagle.

Fish Owls

(right and below) were named because they eat a lot of fish. Many fish owls have fringe on their feathers that reduces wing noise so they can sneak up on fish. They also have spiny tips on their toes that help them hang onto fresh-caught fish while they fly. Fish owls are found in many parts of the world. The owls shown here are from Malaysia.

Monkeys

MONKEY

are primates found in Asia, Africa, Mexico, and Central and South America. Many monkeys are arboreal, which means they spend most of their time high up in trees. Some monkeys have tails they use like extra arms or legs.

Spider Monkeys

See page 39 to learn about spider monkeys.

See page 39 to learn about spider monkeys.

Owl Monkeys

(right) are also called night owls and night monkeys. They have large, owl-like eyes, and hunt for crickets, katydids, moths, and beetles at night.

Lion Tamarins

(right) were named for their lion-like manes. They live in Brazil and are also called "King of the rainforest." There are very few lion tamarins left in the wild, and they are listed as Critically Endangered.

Squirrel Monkeys

(above) spend their days leaping from tree to tree, the way squirrels do, in South and Central American rainforests. They talk with noises that sound like whistles and squeaks.

Seals

are mammals that live in oceans in many places around the world. Females are called cows, and come ashore every year to mate and give birth.

Most seals eat fish, krill, squid, and crabs, although some types, such as the leopard seal, also eat birds.

SEAL

Leopard Seals

(left) live and hunt in the icy waters of the Antarctic. Their fur has a spotted pattern, and they have very sharp teeth for catching prey.

Elephant Seals

Right: See page 22 to learn about elephant seals.

Sea Lions

were named for the lion-like roars they make when talking to each other. Males sometimes roar for hours at a time. Sea lions also make barking sounds. If they ever need another name, we can call them sea dogs!

Snakes

are long, slender reptiles whose bodies are covered in scales. There are more than 2,700 species (types) of snakes and they are found almost everywhere in the world.

SNAKE

SNAKE SCALES

Scales protect a snake's body from injury and allow its skin to stretch when it eats. Snake scales are made from the same material as our fingernails, and they are not slimy.

Gopher Snakes

(right) live in American deserts and use their sense of smell to find mice, lizards, birds, and gophers for food. Gopher snakes are not venomous, but when coyotes, foxes, or large birds try to eat them, they coil up, hiss, and rattle their tails to scare the attacker away.

Parrot Snakes

(left) live in South America. They are bright green with many of the same accent colors as some types of parrots. They live on the forest floor and eat small lizards and frogs.

Fox Snakes

are not venomous. They kill the mice and birds they eat by squeezing them very tight. This type of snake is called a constrictor.

Worm Snakes

(above) are small snakes with smooth scales that look like earthworms. They live under rocks and leaves, and eat earthworms for dinner.

Crayfish Snakes

live under logs and rocks in streams. They earned their name because they eat a lot of crayfish, but they also eat insects, small frogs, and fish.

Tiger Snakes

(above) have colorful black and orange markings on their bodies that look like tiger stripes. They are members of the cobra family, and their bites are venomous. They live in Tasmania and Australia.

Eels

EELS

Eels are a type of fish that live in oceans. Scientists think there are about 600 species (types) of eels. When they are not hunting, most eels hide in caves, crevices, or holes in the sand.

Zebra Moray Eels

are dark brown or black with thin white stripes encircling their bodies. During the day, zebra moray eels hide under rocks and in crevices of coral reefs. At night, they hunt for sea urchins, clams, and crabs.

Tiger Eels

live in the oceans near Australia and Africa. Their bodies are covered with black spots. They spend most of their time hiding, covered in sand, but come out to hunt for small fish.

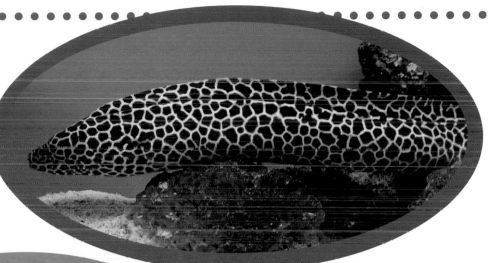

Wolf Eels

(left) are really a type of fish. They live in the oceans from Japan to California, and spend their days hiding in caves from predators and their nights hunting for food. Wolf eels use their strong teeth to eat crabs and mussels, not people!

More Eels Named After Animals:

Mashed Porcupine Eels, Worm Eels, Leopard Eels, & Peacock Eels

Snake Eels

(above right) live in oceans around the world and were named for the snake-like shape of their bodies. Snake eels use their pointed tails to dig holes in the sand, then hide in the holes with only their heads sticking out! There are many types of snake eels, and some of them are named after animals, including the crocodile snake eel and the tiger snake eel.

Sharks

are a type of fish that have skeletons made of cartilage, not bone. To test the difference between bone and cartilage, push on one of the large bones in your arm, then push on the cartilage in your nose or ear.

There are more than 350 different types of sharks. They have the strongest jaws of all animals, and are able to move their upper and lower jaws in different directions at the same time.

Sharks also have LOTS of teeth, and grow a new tooth every time they lose one. Some sharks can go through as many as 20,000 teeth in their lives!

SHARK

SHARK TEETH

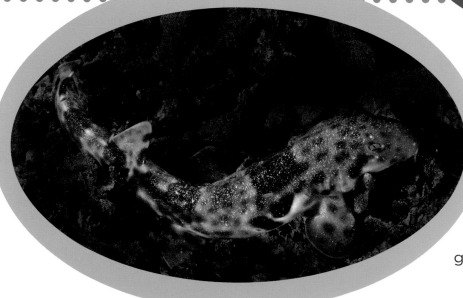

Cat Sharks

(left) have cat-like eyes and live near ocean coastlines. Some have spots and some have stripes. Cat sharks swim together in large groups called schools.

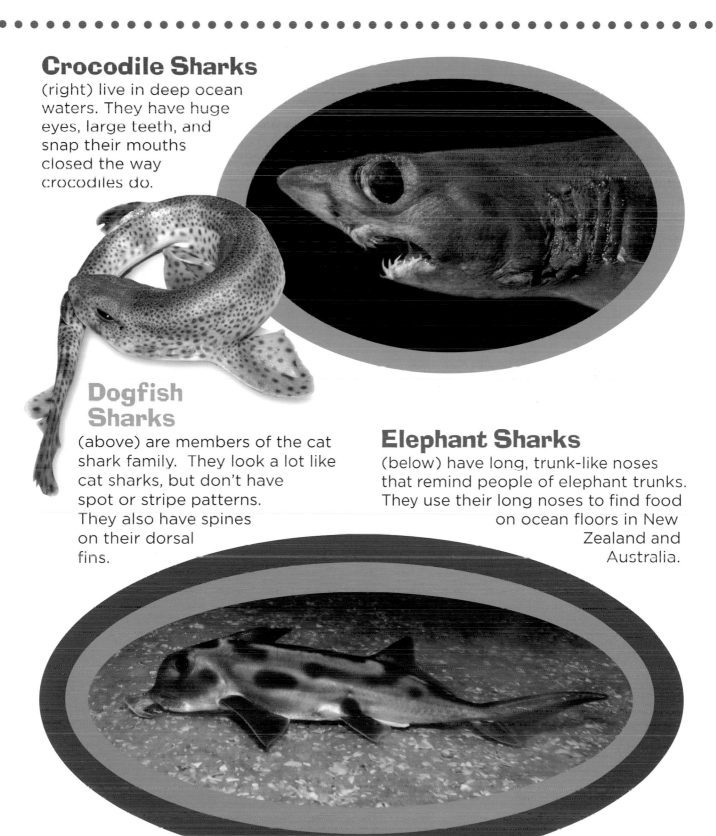

Crocodile Sharks

(right) live in deep ocean waters. They have huge eyes, large teeth, and snap their mouths closed the way crocodiles do.

Dogfish Sharks

(above) are members of the cat shark family. They look a lot like cat sharks, but don't have spot or stripe patterns. They also have spines on their dorsal fins.

Elephant Sharks

(below) have long, trunk-like noses that remind people of elephant trunks. They use their long noses to find food on ocean floors in New Zealand and Australia.

Fox Sharks

were named after foxes because both animals have large tails. Fox sharks catch fish by hitting them with their tails! They are also called thresher sharks.

Whale Sharks

(below) were named after whales because of their large size. In fact, whale sharks are the world's largest fish. Given their large size, some people are surprised to find out whale sharks are mostly vegetarians. They swim with their mouths open and eat small plants and animals that are part of plankton.

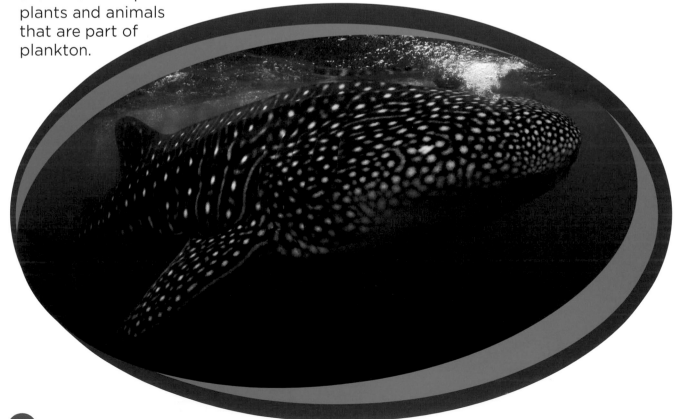

Tiger Sharks

(above) have both stripes and spots. They have big eyes and big mouths, and are one of the few types of sharks known to attack people. They often hunt for fish in shallow waters where people are diving or swimming.

Zebra Sharks

(above) only have stripes when they're young. See page 20 for more info about zebra sharks.

Leopard Sharks

(right) lose their spots as they age. See page 19 to learn more about leopard sharks.

Fish

Fish are found in fresh and salt waters all over the world. If someone showed you 100 animal pictures and asked you to pick out the fish, it would be easy. If someone asked you to describe the traits that make a fish a fish, could you do it?

Fish are vertebrates that live in water. They have scales, are cold blooded, and have fins. Fish also have gills, which are used to bring oxygen into their bodies by moving water over their gills.

FISH

Cowfish

(below) are a type of boxfish that eat algae and small animals. They were named for the two horns near their eyes that look like bull horns. The horns may discourage bigger fish from eating cowfish because the horns make them hard to swallow!

Squirrelfish

(above) have large eyes, just like squirrels, and use them at night to hunt for smaller fish and crabs. During the day, Squirrelfish hide in caves and under reef rocks.

Zebra Lionfish

are in the scorpionfish family. They are also called turkeyfish, dragonfish, and firefish. Lionfish were named for their ferocious look and rows of mane-like stinging spines. Lionfish used to live only in cool Pacific oceans, but a few fish were let go in warmer Caribbean waters, where they have multiplied and caused a lot of damage to coral reef animals.

Porcupinefish

(left) are a type of pufferfish named for the long spines found all over their bodies. They are also called hedge-hog fish. There are more than 130 species (types) of pufferfish.

Dog-Faced Pufferfish

(right) were named for their dog-like look. Pufferfish do not have scales, which may help the dog-face puffer look more like a family pet than a fish!

Frogfish

(this page) have lumpy, loose-fitting skin, much like toad skin.

Frogfish are known for the amazing way they hunt. Instead of chasing prey, frogfish have a body part that looks like a hurt worm or fish. When a curious fish comes over for what looks like a tasty treat, the frogfish sucks them in!

Most frogfish blend in very well with their backgrounds, which helps them trick more prey fish.

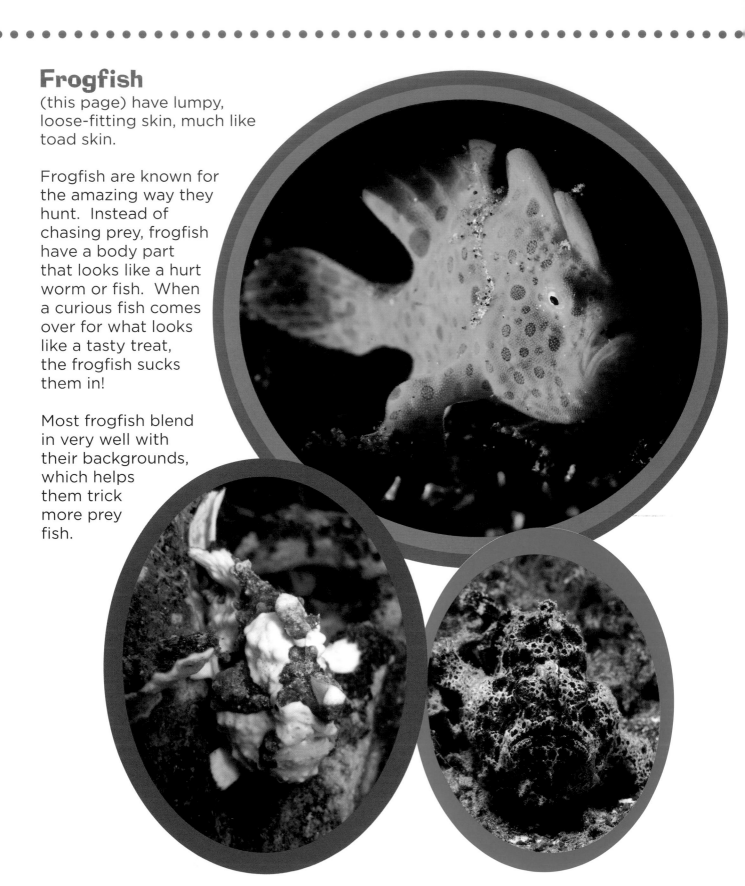

Hawkfish

(right) were named after hawks because their hunting techniques are similar to the way hawk birds hunt. Hawkfish wait on the tallest area of a coral reef. When they see a possible dinner fish come by, they swoop down and grab them.

Scorpionfish

(above and right) blend in with rocks and coral around them while waiting for an unsuspecting dinner fish to swim by. There are many types of scorpionfish, and the photo above shows a devil scorpionfish. See page 37 to learn more about scorpionfish.

Butterflyfish

(left) were named for their colorful fins that flutter like butterflies. They live near coral reefs and eat small invertebrates. Some butterflyfish also have eye-spots on their fins to confuse predators, just like some butterflies do.

Raccoon Butterflyfish

(right) have black markings that look like a raccoon's mask, and are also known as crescent-marked butterflyfish. They hunt at night in small schools in shallow reefs.

Goatfish

(left) were named for the goat-like whiskers (called barbels) on their chins. Goatfish, like catfish, use their barbels to find food.

Jaguar Cichlids

(right) were named for their black spots and large canine teeth. They are fierce predators, eating small fish and fresh-water worms.

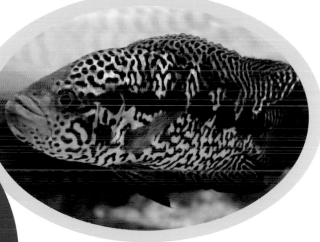

Rabbitfish

(left) are also known as bunnyfish. They were named for their rabbit-like grazing of algae on rock surfaces. They are valued because their algae grazing helps keep coral reefs healthy.

Foxface Rabbitfish

(right) live in the Pacific Ocean near Indonesia. They were named for the fox-like markings on their faces.

Hippo Tang

(left) have many common names, including blue tang and doctorfish. They may have been named after hippos because they graze on algae, the same way hippos graze on plants.

Batfish

Left: See page 30 to learn about batfish.

Parrotfish

(right) were named for their parrot-like beaks, which are formed by a cluster of teeth. They use their beaks to scrape algae from coral and rocks.

Eel-Catfish

(left) were named after eels because of their long, thin bodies. They use their barbels (the whisker-like hairs near their mouths) to stir up the sandy bottoms of reefs and rivers while searching for small worms, crabs, mollusks, and fish.

Catfish

Above: Catfish earned their name for the long, whisker-like barbels on their faces. There are many types of catfish.

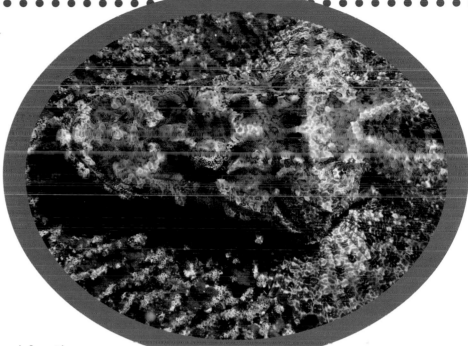

Crocodilefish

(above right) were named for the crocodile-like shape of their snouts. They live in the reefs of the Western Pacific oceans, and hide themselves from predators by blending in with the ocean floor. Crocodilefish eat small fish, not people!

Ratfish

Above: See page 31 to learn about ratfish.

Mosquitofish

(above) are small fish that are loved by health departments because each fish can eat dozens of mosquito larvae every day. That's the good news. The bad news is that they will also eat small, endangered fish so people have to be very careful where they put them.

Birdmouth Wrasse

(left) were named because their mouths are shaped like bird beaks. Their pointed mouths help them find food in small places in coral reefs. They are also called bird wrasse and blackbird wrasse.

Pigfish

(below) were named because they grunt like pigs. Pigfish make the sound by rubbing their teeth together! They usually grunt only when disturbed by a predator.

Snakeheads

Above: See page 35 to learn about snakeheads.

Lizardfish

(right and below) have lizard-like bodies and heads, and lots of teeth. Lizardfish hide under the sand on the ocean floor with only their eyes sticking out, then attack unsuspecting prey when they swim nearby.

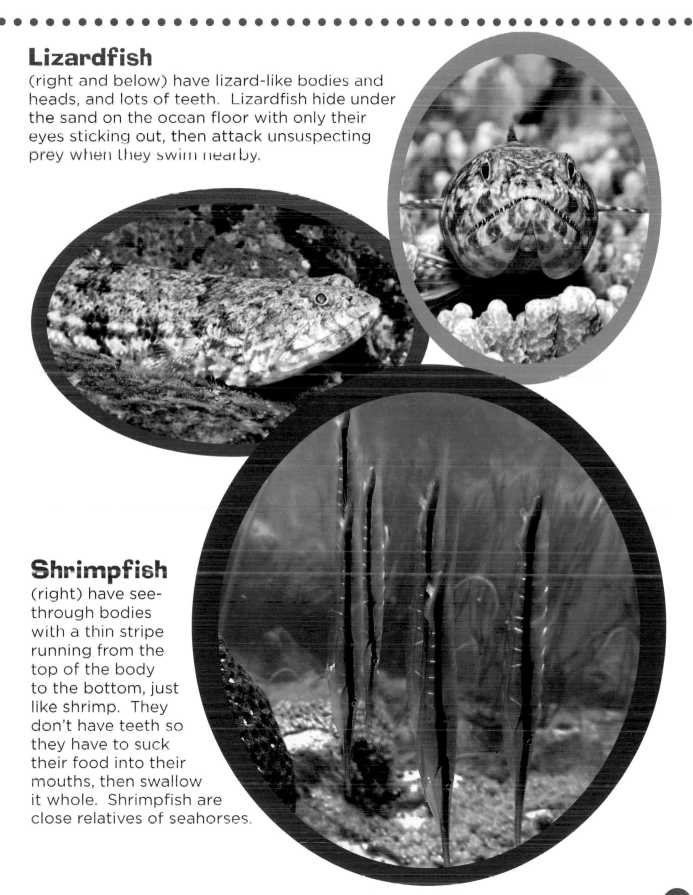

Shrimpfish

(right) have see-through bodies with a thin stripe running from the top of the body to the bottom, just like shrimp. They don't have teeth so they have to suck their food into their mouths, then swallow it whole. Shrimpfish are close relatives of seahorses.

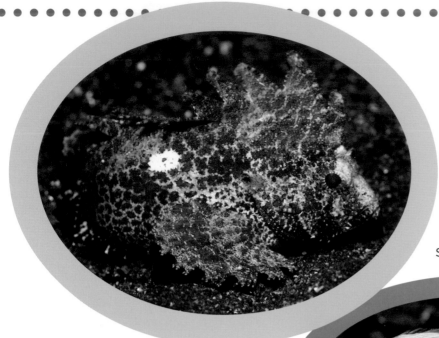

Waspfish

(left) were named for the strong toxin in their spines that stings like a wasp bite. They live in deep waters of the Indian and West Pacific Oceans. They hunt by resting on the ocean floor, preying on small crabs and fish.

Zebra Surgeonfish

(right) were named for their zebra-like stripes. The stripes help them blend in with their coral reef habitat.

Houndfish

(above) are a group of fish found in deep waters in the Red Sea, the Indian Ocean and the Mediterranean Sea. They are also called needlefish, after their pointed snouts, and one species is called the crocodile needlefish.

Toadfish

(right) were named for the toad-like sounds they make with their swim bladders. Toadfish are ambush predators, hiding under sand and seaweed until they see a fish they want to eat.

Clown Skunkfish

(left) were named after skunks because of the skunk-like white stripe that runs down their backs.

More Fish Named After Animals:

Ponyfish, Sheepshead Fish, Goosefish, Wormfish, Snailfish, Viperfish, & Roosterfish

Name Games

1. Can you find hints of common names in scientific names?

You may have noticed that one animal can have many different common names. Animals usually have only one scientific name, though. Scientific names contain the genus and the species information, and are usually written in italics. Look up the scientific names of the animals named after tigers on pages 10-17. How many of them have tiger in part of their scientific name?

2. Which type of animal inspires the most cool animal names?

Write down the types of animals (amphibians, birds, etc.) listed in purple on the index pages, then count the number of animals in each group. Which type of animal wins?

3. Which size of animal inspires the most cool animal names?

Make a photocopy of the table of contents pages. Circle all of the animals that you would describe as "large animals" in red and all of the animals you would describe as "small animals" in blue. Look through the book and count the number of large and small animals named after other animals. Which size animal wins?

4. Solve these animal name mysteries!

Research the animals below and the buffalo treehopper on page 5 to find out why they were named after other animals. Were you surprised by what you found out? Show the photos to some friends and see if they can guess how these animals received their names.

Panther Chameleon

Sea Wasp

Zebra Beetle

Flamingo Tongue Snail

Index

ACKNOWLEDGMENTS

Gratitude is extended to the following individuals and institutions: Gary Albrecht, Will Albrecht, Dr. Stanislav Gorb, Catherine Ham, Dr. Ronald Ham, Joseph K. H. Koh, Peggy Greb-USDA (page 50), Dr. Tim Forrest, Stephen Kajiura (page 63, top right, © copyright Stephen Kajiura / SeaPics.com), Jan Meerman, Charles Nurnberg, Joanne O'Sullivan, David L. Pearson, and Alfried P. Vogler; Bigstock Photo, Istock Photo, Shutterstock; Burke Museum (Herpetology Department), Fir0002 Flagstaffotos.com.au (pages 23 and 63-http://en.wikipedia.org/wiki/Wikipedia:Text_of_the_GNU_Free_Documentation_License), Fishbase.org, Florida Museum of Natural History (Ichthyology Department), Marinebio.org, National Geographic, North Carolina Aquariums, Royal Alberta Museum, San Diego Zoo, Theprayingmantis.org, Types-of-spiders.org.uk, Singapore Science Centre, and Vancouver Aquarium.